MEDUSA AND PEGASUS

AMY HAYES

Cavendish Square
New York

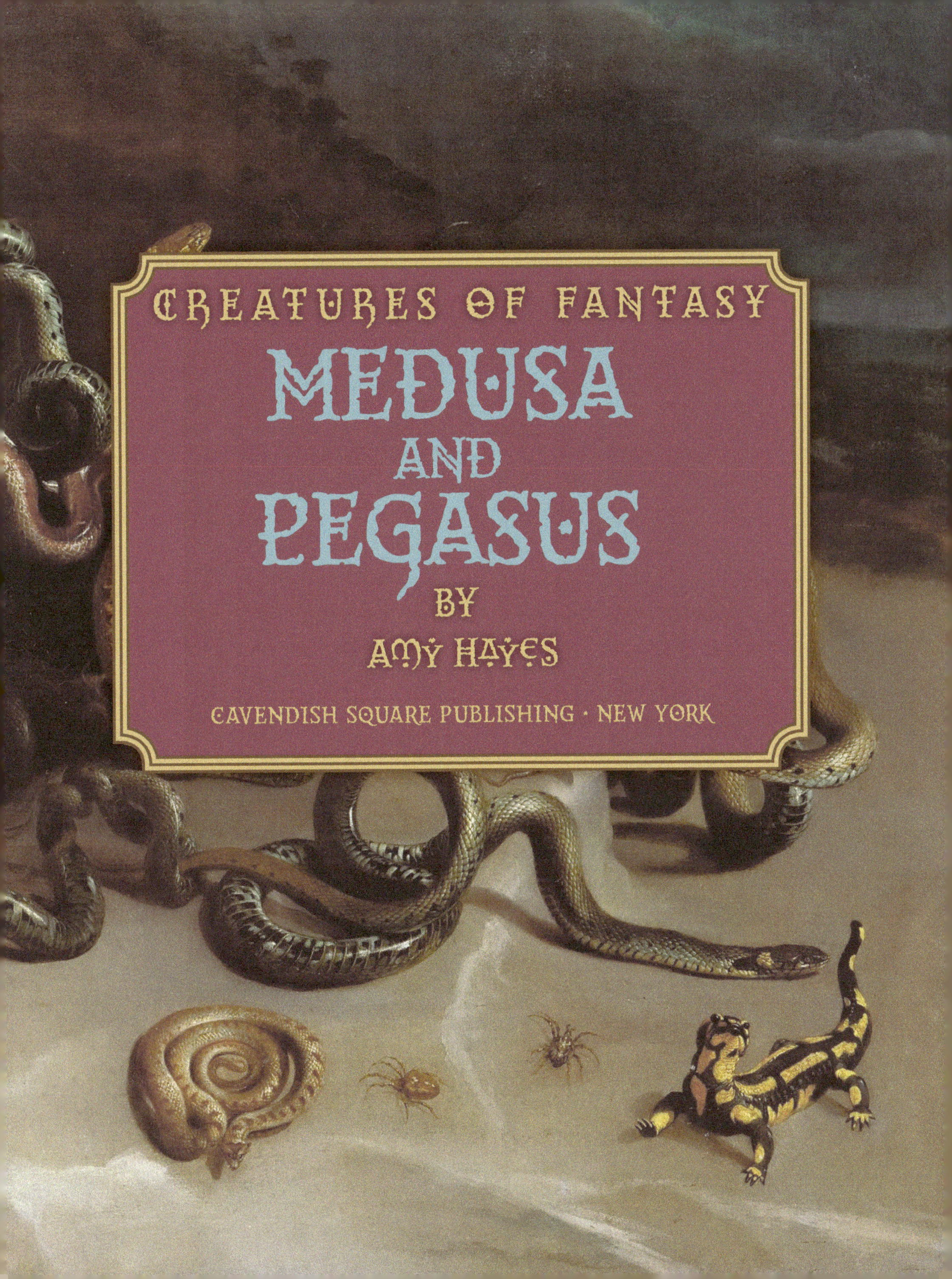

CREATURES OF FANTASY

MEDUSA AND PEGASUS

BY

AMY HAYES

CAVENDISH SQUARE PUBLISHING · NEW YORK

For my grandfather, Pliny the Elder.

Published in 2016 by Cavendish Square Publishing, LLC
243 5th Avenue, Suite 136, New York, NY 10016

First Edition

Cataloging-in-Publication Data

Hayes, Amy.
Medusa and Pegasus / by Amy Hayes.
p. cm. — (Creatures of fantasy)
Includes index.
ISBN 978-1-50260-506-1 (hardcover) ISBN 978-1-50260-507-8 (ebook)
1. Medusa (Greek mythology) — Juvenile literature. 2. Pegasus (Greek mythology) — Juvenile literature.
3. Perseus (Greek mythology) — Juvenile literature. I. Hayes, Amy. II. Title.
BL820.M38 H39 2016
398.20938'01—d23

Editorial Director: David McNamara
Editor: Kristen Susienka
Copy Editor: Rebecca Rohan
Art Director: Jeffrey Talbot
Designer: Joseph Macri
Senior Production Manager: Jennifer Ryder-Talbot
Production Editor: Renni Johnson
Photo Research: J8 Media

The photographs in this book are used by permission and through the courtesy of: File:Peter Paul Rubens - Perseus and Andromeda (Hermitage Museum).jpg/Wikimedia Commons, cover; Peter Paul Rubens (public domain) File: Rubens Medusa.jpeg/Wikimedia Commons, title page; Christiana Stawski/Moment Open/Getty Images, introduction; S. Vannini/De Agostini Picture Library/Getty Images, 9; Eye Ubiquitous/UIG/Getty Images, 12; Photoservice Electa/Universal Images Group/Superstock, 14; File: Edward Burne-Jones Public Domain/The Finding of Medusa, 1882.jpg /Wikimedia Commons, 15; Private Collection/Bridgeman Images, 19; Private Collection / The Stapleton Collection /Bridgeman Images, 21; Peter Willi/SuperStock, 22; Mondadori Portfolio/Getty Images, 24; Rhkamen/Moment/Getty Images, 27; Dr. K/File: Close up of Gorgon at the pediment of Artemis temple in Corfu.jpg /Wikimedia Commons, 29; Walt Disney Pictures/Bray, Phil /Album/Newscom, 30; Southampton City Art Gallery, Hampshire, UK/Bridgeman Images, 32; Ardea/Radi, Giacomo /Animals Animals, 35; A. DAGLI ORTI/De Agostini Picture Library/Getty Images, 36; File: La Parnasse, by Andrea Mantegna, from C2RMF retouched.jpg/Wikimedia Commons, 38; David Ohmer/Moment/Getty Images, 40; British Library, London, UK / Bridgeman Images, 41; Private Collection/Bridgeman Images, 44; Museo Archeologico, Florence, Italy/Bridgeman Images, 48; Culture Club/Getty Images, 50; Private Collection/The Stapleton Collection/Bridgeman Images, 51; A. Dagli Orti/De Agostini Picture Library/Getty Images, 52; Private Collection/Archives Charmet/Bridgeman Images, 56; Juniors/Superstock, (top) Walt Disney Pictures/Ronald Grant Archive/Alamy, (bottom) 57; Jay Pasachoff/Superstock, 58.

Printed in the United States of America

CONTENTS

Pegasus was a mythical winged horse that flew through the clouds.

Introduction

Since the first humans walked Earth, myths and legends have engaged minds and inspired imaginations. Ancient civilizations used stories to explain phenomena in the world around them: the weather, tides, and natural disasters. As different cultures evolved, so too did their stories. From their traditions and observations emerged creatures with powerful abilities, mythical intrigue, and their own origins. Sometimes, different cultures encouraged various manifestations of the same creature. At other times, these creatures and cultures morphed into entirely new beings with greater powers than their predecessors.

Today, societies still celebrate the folklore of their ancestors—in films such as *The Hobbit, Maleficent,* and *X-Men*; and in books such as the Harry Potter and Lightning Thief series. Some even believe creatures from these stories truly existed, and continue to walk the earth as living creatures. Others resign these beings to myth.

In the Creatures of Fantasy series, we celebrate captivating stories of the past from all around the world. Each book focuses on creatures both familiar and unknown: the cunning leprechaun, the valiant Pegasus, the cursed werewolf, and the towering giant. Their various incarnations throughout history are brought to life. All have their own origins, their own legends, and their own influences on the imagination today. Each story adds a new perspective to the human experience, and encourages people to revisit tales of the past in order to understand their presence in the modern age.

1

THE SNAKE-HAIRED MONSTER

"On all sides, through the fields, along the highways,
He saw the forms of men and beasts, made stone
By one look at Medusa's face."
OVID, THE *METAMORPHOSES,* TRANS. ROLFE HUMPHRIES

OF ALL THE TERRIBLE MONSTERS THAT appear in Greek **mythology**, none has sparked more imagination than Medusa. Just one look at her hideous face could turn a person to stone, and she is known for her terrible head of snakes. Her story has been passed down through the ages from the Greeks to modern day. Her name has become as widely known as Heracles (Hercules), Zeus, and even her enemies, Athene (Athena) and Perseus. Though her story has changed from teller to teller, her serpentine hair has remained a symbol of her powers.

Opposite: Medusa's head of snakes decorates the door of Chateau de la Roche Courbon, Saint-Porchaire.

The First Medusa

The first recorded mention of Medusa is by Homer, who lived in Greece around 750 BCE. Homer was a storyteller who travelled across the country, telling his grand tales by firelight to captive audiences. Although he is considered an author, usually he didn't invent his own stories. Instead, Homer recited many tales he had learned on his travels, or that his elders had passed on to him. Instead of writing them down, he had to remember all of the stories from memory because he was blind. Homer was a great storyteller, and compiled two **epics**, or long tales that include many little stories. The epics he created are called the *Odyssey* and the *Iliad*. In the *Iliad*, he mentions the horrible face of Medusa "with her stare of horror."

Homer does not spend much more time explaining Medusa, but instead he goes on to describe Athene. It might seem strange that in the first mention we have of Medusa, she is barely talked about. However, stories were told over and over again in ancient Greece. By the time Homer began his storytelling, Medusa was already a scary monster that haunted nightmares. Her story was well known before the first myths of ancient Greece were being recorded in writing.

The first telling of Medusa will always be shrouded in mystery. Like many folktales and myths, the origin of her story has been lost to time. Another reason why we don't know the author of the original Medusa tale is because she is part of Greek mythology. To the people of ancient Greece, myths were more than just fairy tales and stories. They were also a part of Greek religion. The Greeks were **polytheistic**, and the gods and goddesses who played a major part in these tales were worshipped in Greece at the time. The story of Medusa was repeated not only for the listeners' enjoyment, but also to remind them of the powers of the gods and the respect they deserved.

Snake Siblings

The origins of Medusa have changed over time, but the oldest tales have some commonalities. One of them was that Medusa was one of the three **Gorgon** sisters. They were the daughters of Phorcys, an ancient sea god, and Ceto (Keto), his sea monster sister. According to myth, Phorcys and Ceto existed before the gods and even before their previous overlords, the Titans.

The Gorgons had several siblings, including Echidna, Ladon, and the Graea. Echidna and Ladon were both horrible snake monsters who lived in the ocean, while the Graea—also called the Gray Maids—were three sisters born with hair as gray as an old woman's. Many believe that these monstrous children were supposed to represent the risks of the sea. Descendants of sea gods, they were often described with water imagery: the Graea with tendrils of gray hair like the foam of waves; the Gorgons with their lolling tongues like streams or rivers. Another reason for this conclusion is that the siblings resided in the ocean, or beyond it. Rather than saying directly that the sea was dangerous, it was more exciting for the Greeks to **personify** the sea as different monsters, ready to kill unsuspecting adventurers.

There is another, later Medusa origin story told by the playwright Euripides. According to his play *Ion*, Ge, the mother goddess and goddess of the earth, brought forth the Gorgons to aid her children, the giants, in a war against the gods. Ge had been jealous of Zeus and had persuaded the giants to attack Olympus. Giants in Greek myths had hot tempers and were known to throw rocks and tree trunks. They varied in description from story to story, but it is generally agreed that they had legs that ended with the tails of snakes. Perhaps this is another link to Medusa: wherever she is mentioned, she is related somehow to snakes.

Grim Gorgons

In most of the Greek myths, there were only three Gorgons. Their names were Stheno, Euryale, and Medusa. They lived by themselves on a lonely island beyond a large desert and past the Mediterranean Sea. Anyone who dared to come to the island was quickly turned to stone by looking at a Gorgon's face. As a result, the three sisters lived among statues, animals, and people who were forever frozen in place.

The Gorgons were gruesome creatures. Each sister had boars' tusks for teeth, snakes for hair, and bronze hands with sharp claws.

The three Gorgon sisters are represented here at the Secession Building in Vienna, Austria.

They also had wings of gold, and red tongues that hung from their mouths. They were very strong and practically impossible to kill. Stheno and Euryale were immortal and ageless, which meant that they could not grow old or die. Medusa, however, was mortal. Her powers of turning others to stone, though, made it impossible for anyone to kill her without help from the gods.

A Rationalist's View

Not all Greeks believed the story of the mythical monster with snakes for hair. A group of philosophers called the **rationalists** became very influential in Greece, and they were determined that the world could be understood by logic and reason. While they appreciated the stories of the gods, rationalists preferred logic over magic and myths, and changed the stories to fit their ideals.

In a tale by Palaephatus, a rationalist who lived in the fourth century BCE, Phorcys was not a sea god but a man who owned three islands and a beautiful golden statue of Athene. When he died, he distributed his islands to his three daughters, Stheno, Euryale, and Medusa. The three sisters each took turns protecting the golden statue, which was called a Gorgon.

A statue of the goddess Athene

How Medusa Lost Her Looks

Every time a story is told, it changes slightly. After a while, a story can become very different from its origins. This happened to the story of Medusa many times. Sometimes a change can become an important part of the story and alter its meaning completely. This is the recording of one such instance.

Around 200 BCE, a scholar known as Apollodorus was said to have written a history of heroes called *The Library*. According to *The Library*, and many later storytellers, Medusa was once a beautiful maiden who was much loved by everyone. Her finest feature was her beautiful long hair. Many suitors came to court Medusa, but she would have none of them. Even gods fell in love with her. Poseidon, the sea god, finally captured the favors of Medusa while she was worshipping in the temple of the goddess Athene.

When Athene discovered that Poseidon and Medusa had been together in her temple, she was furious. She decided to punish Medusa, who "was fain to match herself with the goddess even in beauty," meaning that Medusa thought she was prettier than Athene. It was always dangerous for a mortal to compare themselves to a god. Athene, angry that Medusa believed she was prettier than the goddess, decided to take her revenge. She cursed Medusa with the hideous looks of a Gorgon, and ensured the next man to look at her would turn to stone.

PERSEUS AND MEDUSA

" . . . there suddenly stood three infernal Furies flecked with blood, who had the limbs of women and their ways / but wore as girdles, snakes of the deepest green; small serpents and horned vipers formed their hairs . . . "

DANTE ALIGHIERI, *INFERNO*, TRANS. ALLEN MANDELBAUM

MANY GREEK MYTHS BEGIN WITH THE ending of a different tale and end as the beginning of another. The tale of Perseus slaying Medusa is no different. In order to understand the story, we first must go back a generation and learn the story of Perseus's mother, Danaë.

The Fate of Danaë

Danaë was a princess born to Acrisius, king of Argos. Acrisius was never a loving father, but he treated Danaë fairly. One day an **oracle** had a vision of the future and told Acrisius a horrible truth: that he would be murdered by his grandson. To keep this from happening, Acrisius decided to prevent Danaë from ever

Opposite: Edward Burne-Jones's *The Perseus Series: The Finding of Medusa*

having children, and locked her up in a prison away from everyone. However, once a prophecy is told, it will come true, be it by the actions of mortals or gods. Zeus, knowing how unfair and lonely it was to be imprisoned in a tower, took pity on Danaë and decided to visit her as a ray of sunshine shimmering in through the keyhole of her locked cell. Soon Danaë was with child.

Horrified that the prophecy might come true, Acrisius forced Danaë and her infant, Perseus, into a wooden trunk and threw it out to sea. Instead of sinking, however, the chest floated, and after several days the mother and son washed ashore on the island of Seriphos. A handsome fisherman named Dictys rescued them, and Danaë quickly fell in love with him. Unfortunately, Dictys's older brother, Polydectes, was the king of the island. He had noticed Danaë's beauty, and demanded that she be his wife.

Danaë refused to marry Polydectes, but with no home to return to, she decided to join his household as a servant instead. Polydectes would not give up his quest to marry Danaë, however. As time wore on, he hoped she would agree to become his wife, and no longer be forced to be a servant. But Danaë was **steadfast**. Polydectes grew bitter and even became jealous of Perseus, who Danaë always showered with motherly affection. As Perseus grew, Polydectes took him on as a servant as well, and delighted in chastising and embarrassing him. Perseus was a prideful young man, and Polydectes hatched a plan to get rid of Perseus once and for all.

Polydectes's Ploy

Polydectes told his subjects that he was engaged to a noble woman who lived in a faraway kingdom. In ancient Greece it was common to give a man gifts to honor an upcoming marriage, so that he may impress his bride's family. Polydectes asked his friends to bring him as many horses as they could spare. His friends and relatives presented him with many beautiful and strong horses, but Perseus, who was poor, could not bring him anything. When Polydectes was surrounded by friends, he scorned Perseus for his stinginess. Embarrassed and angry, Perseus vowed to go on a quest and bring the king anything he desired. He had fallen into Polydectes's trap. Polydectes, overjoyed that his plan had worked, asked for the most dangerous present he could think of: the head of a Gorgon.

The Nymphai bestow the helmet of invisibility upon Perseus.

Perseus could not go back on his promise, but his heart was heavy. He had been tricked, and now he would have to face the dreaded Gorgons. He knew he would probably die. That night, he went to the temple of Athene, the goddess of wisdom and war. He prayed and asked for her guidance in his quest. Athene heard his prayer and decided to help Perseus. She appeared to Perseus in the temple.

The Quest Begins

Athene guided Perseus to the Greae, who would help him find the Nymphai, or nymphs. The nymphs' powers could help him find Medusa. The Greae possessed great knowledge, but they had only one tooth and one eye among them. To see and to talk, they passed the tooth and eye to one another. When Perseus arrived, he tricked one of the sisters into handing him the eye, placing his strong, firm hand where a thin, old one should be. Once he held the eye, he refused to give it back until they told him where to find the Nymphai, or nymphs. Unable to see, the three **crones** bartered information for the eye and told Perseus what he needed to know, and he was soon on his way.

Perseus then visited the nymphs, who lived in a garden where the sun always shines and golden apples grow on trees. He told them of his quest to kill one of the monstrous Gorgons. Nymphs hate creatures of darkness and are happy to follow the will of the gods. With Athene on his side, the nymphs gladly agreed to help Perseus. In order to defeat Medusa, the nymphs gave Perseus three magical possessions. The first gift was the helmet of Hades, the god of the dead. With this gift Perseus would be invisible to all who looked on him, allowing him to sneak up on the Gorgons. The second gift was the golden sandals of Hermes, the winged messenger god. These sandals gave Perseus the gift of flight, making it possible for Perseus to fly as fast as the wind. The third gift of the Nymphai was a *kibisis,* a silver sack with golden tassels. This would hold the Gorgon's head.

Some say that Athene gave Perseus her own sword to slay the Gorgon. Others say it was Hermes's sword, for no mortal sword could slay Medusa: her blood was so poisonous it would melt any sword that cut her. This sword was kept in a sheath of darkness, and when Perseus drew it, he saw that it glowed. Finally, Athene gave Perseus a shield so smooth and perfect that he could see his own reflection in it. Prepared for battle, he made his way to the island of the Gorgons.

The Gorgon's Head

Perseus sneaks up on Medusa.

Perseus flew over the Libyan Desert, across faraway lands, and beyond the great ocean. He flew until finally he reached the island of the Gorgons. He landed quietly on the shore, surrounded by statues of unlucky sailors who had been turned to stone. He crept softly, listening for any hint of noise, prepared to shut his eyes at a moment's notice. As he continued to walk along the rocky shore, he brought out his shield and looked through its clear surface to guide his path. Through the mirror-shield he saw several warriors, their weapons held out in battle, their faces **petrified** in expressions of horror.

Perseus followed the trail of statues until he found a mass of stone creatures surrounding a rock cliff. Warriors, sailors, deer, and even trees were stone, as they all had succumbed to the horrible sight of a Gorgon's face. Perseus closed his eyes in fear. He knew that the Gorgons must live at the bottom of the cliff. He brought his shield to his face and kept it close, walking backwards so he could see through the reflection what came ahead. Eventually he came across the three Gorgon sisters asleep under the cliff. Again he closed his eyes, but he was not turned to stone. He had not looked upon the Gorgons, but had seen their reflections in the shield.

Careful not to look away from the shield, he moved toward the Gorgons. As he saw the hideous reflection of Medusa, he brought out his glowing sword. Athene guided it true, and Perseus cut off Medusa's head, which let out a terrible shriek. The two other Gorgons woke snarling, and were horrified to see their sister dead beside them.

Perseus raises the head of Medusa against his enemies at Seriphos.

They jumped up, ready to attack the killer, but they could see no one. Perseus, wearing Hades's helmet, was invisible to them.

Perseus quickly put the head of Medusa inside the silver sack and flew off, over the ocean, the Libyan Desert, and the sea toward Argos. All was not well, however. With Perseus gone, there was no one to protect his mother Danaë from Polydectes. In order to avoid being forced into marriage, she fled to Dictys, and the two hid in the temple of the gods. Perseus heard of his mother's plight and returned to Seriphos. When he arrived, Polydectes was enraged, for he had hoped to never see Perseus again. Polydectes set his guards upon him.

Perseus, furious that Polydectes had sent him off to die on what should have been an impossible task, and horrified that his mother had been forced into hiding, raised the kibisis. "You asked me for the head of a Gorgon," he said. "I hope you like your wedding present!" Averting his eyes, he brought the head of Medusa out of its sack and turned his enemies to stone.

Between a Rock and a Hard Place

As Perseus was flying back to Seriphos over the Mediterranean Sea, he came across a strange sight. A large rock jutted out from the sea, and he saw a young woman chained to the rock, quaking in fear as the water rose higher with the tides.

Perseus found the woman so beautiful he nearly forgot to flap the wings of his borrowed sandals. He flew down to her and asked her who she was. The woman told him that her name was Andromeda, the daughter of the king of Ethiopia and his wife Cassiopeia. Cassiopeia had angered the gods by comparing her own beauty to godliness, and as punishment, Andromeda must die.

Andromeda had not even finished her story when a terrifying roar came from behind Perseus. A giant sea monster appeared atop the crest of a huge wave. It began to head straight for the rock. Perseus could see Andromeda's parents grieving by the shore. He flew over to them. He told them that he would save Andromeda and fight off the sea monster, but in exchange for such a dangerous task, he wanted to marry Andromeda, for he had fallen in love with her. Terrified for their daughter, the couple agreed, and Perseus returned to fight off the sea monster.

Perseus fought the sea monster, dashing back and forth between the waves. Finally, he delivered a deathblow, and the victory was his. He broke Andromeda's chains and brought her to shore, and the couple married soon after.

3

MEDUSA'S FATE

"The son of Danaë, Perseus, who slew the Gorgo,
and brought her head wreathed with its serpent locks
to strike stony death to the islanders."
PINDAR, *PYTHIAN ODE* TRANS. G. S. CONWAY

MEDUSA HAS BECOME ONE OF THE MOST famous monsters in Greek mythology. However, she plays a minor role in her own story. The story of Medusa is actually the story of the heroic acts of Perseus. Why, then, if she is just a monster is she so well remembered?

More Than a Monster

An important part of the Medusa story is that she does not lose her deadly powers once she has been killed. Even though she has died, she is still a part of the story. For one thing, she is not left on her island to be buried by her sisters. Her head was requested as a trophy, and so Perseus takes it with him. Once he does that,

Opposite: Caravaggio's famous painting of Medusa's head mounted on a shield.

however, Medusa's role changes. She is no longer a horrible monster of darkness, but a tool that Perseus uses against the evil Polydectes.

In some endings of the story, Perseus uses the head of Medusa to kill his foes, and then presents it to Athene. Athene in turn places the head on her shield. By putting the head of Medusa on her shield, Athene ensures that all her enemies who see it will be turned to stone. The head becomes a form of protection. Medusa transforms in the story from a monster to a tool used by Perseus to finally a symbol of protection and a **sigil** of Athene. This makes Medusa a particularly fascinating character to consider. Is she really evil, or does her power enable her to become a weapon for good?

An Irresistible Face

Even something insignificant can become fascinating if we know that it is forbidden or dangerous. This is a common theme through folktales and mythology, perhaps most famously explored in the Biblical story of the forbidden apple in Genesis, but also in many cautionary tales, such as the woods in "Little Red Riding Hood."

In Medusa's story, many were intrigued by the idea of a face that could turn the viewer to stone. How horrible would that face have to be? As soon as people heard the story, they tried to imagine what Medusa's face could look like. Learning what Medusa looks like is something of a catch-22, however. Since her face turns people to stone, listeners are curious about what they would see. But if a person actually saw the face, the horrible consequences of seeing Medusa would kill them. The tension that is created by a listener wanting to know what Medusa looks like and not wanting to be turned to stone is part of why the story has lived on.

Could Medusa be beautiful?

Paralyzing Beauty

As the story was told over and over again, people continued to **extrapolate** the features of Medusa's face. Because no one (except Perseus through his mirrored shield) could look at her without turning to stone, her appearance has remained a mystery. The idea was so interesting that Medusa's story was changed and talked about through the centuries. Lucian, a writer from the second century, completely reinterpreted the story of the Gorgons and reimagined their horrible looks:

> The beauty of the Gorgons, being extremely powerful and affecting the very vitals of the soul, stunned its beholders and made them speechless, so that, as the story has it and everyone says, they turned to stone in wonder.

Christine de Pizan, a medieval French poet and historian, continued this examination over a thousand years later, writing that the overpowering view of the Gorgons stemmed from beauty:

> This Medusa, according to the ancient stories, was of such striking beauty that not only did she surpass all other women—which was an amazing and supernatural thing ... [but] every mortal creature upon whom she looked ... she seemed to make them immovable. For this reason the fable claimed that they had turned to stone. (trans. Earl Jeffrey Richards)

Pizan takes after the rationalists, focusing less on the mythical aspects of Medusa and more on the effect Medusa has on the person who sees her. The feeling that Pizan talks about is similar to the idea of being **awestruck**, in which a person sees something so amazing or terrifying that they are speechless. She does not think the viewer is turned to stone, but rather that they become powerless as they are overwhelmed by Medusa's beauty.

Many people have described terror at seeing something beautiful, or displaying fear of attraction to another person. This interpretation of Medusa as beautiful is this kind of terror in the extreme—that a person sees something so beautiful they freeze—and even become petrified.

An Artist's Rendering

Through the ages, artists have presented the woman with snakes for hair again and again. Imagining and capturing a creature whose appearance is so linked to her power has enticed many artists. Medusa was clearly a popular figure to represent in ancient Greece, as she appeared regularly on vases and in sculptures. One of the earliest representations of her is the *Temple of Artemis,* dating back to 600 BCE, which shows Medusa in a **frieze** baring her teeth.

Medusa the Gorgon at the Temple of Artemis

However, as the myth of Medusa evolved, so did the way she was depicted. Medusa herself symbolized a monster, but Medusa's head on a shield, for example, represented the protecting power of Athene. As storytellers began to question whether Medusa was ugly or beautiful, so did artists. Medusa has been painted by Caravaggio, Leonardo da Vinci, Salvador Dalí, and many other artists. Each has their own interpretation. Caravaggio's *Medusa* screams in horror, with blood streaming from her neck, while one of the oldest sculptures of Medusa, the *Medusa Rodanini*, shows her as beautiful, the Gorgon snakes and wings only adding to her beauty.

C. S. Lewis's White Witch and Medusa have many similarities.

Medusa: The Witch of Narnia?

"She calls herself the Queen of Narnia though she has no right to be queen at all ... And she can turn people into stone," so Lucy describes the White Witch to her brother Edmund in the book *The Lion, the Witch, and the Wardrobe* by C. S. Lewis. Beautiful but as cold as ice, the Queen has brought everlasting winter to Narnia. Winter is often used in literature as a metaphor for death, and the creatures she turns to stone are lifeless, unable to move. The White Queen is the evil that the children and their animal friends must defeat so that Narnia can become beautiful again.

There are many parallels to Greek mythology in Lewis's story. Fauns and satyrs, Greek mythological creatures, play important roles in the book, particularly Mr. Tumnus, a faun. The lonely island of the Gorgons is also recreated at the entrance to the White Queen's castle. Stone statues litter the landscape: "As he got into the middle of it he saw that there were dozens of statues all about—standing here and there rather as the pieces stand on a chess board when it is half way through the game. There were stone satyrs, and stone wolves, and bears and foxes and cat-a-mountains of stone."

The White Queen has Medusa-like powers that let her turn her enemies into stone. Unlike Medusa, she has control over her power and attacks only those who have angered her. Though beautiful, she is evil and deadly, and the children avoid her at all costs. Did C. S. Lewis get his inspiration for such a terrible villain from the Greek myth? It is quite possible.

CHRY
SAOR
PERSEVS
MEDVSA

MAGICAL BLOOD AND MYTHICAL BIRTHS

"From her blood Pegasus is said to have been born, shaped in the form of renown . . . "
FULGENTIUS, FROM *MYTHOLOGIES*, TRANS. LESLIE G. WHITEBREAD

THE STORY OF PERSEUS SHOWS PERSEUS as a **mythic hero**. He enlists the help of the gods and conquers the evil monster, and his human enemies as well. The story of Perseus is simple, but the story of Medusa is not. Consequences of Medusa's death ripple throughout the world of Greek mythology. Many have to do with her severed head and the trip that Perseus takes from the islands of the Gorgons back to Seriphos.

MAGIC BLOOD

According to Euripides's play *Ion*, Gorgons' blood was imbued with special powers. In the play, the character Cruesa tells an old man

Opposite: The Death of Medusa I by Edward Burne-Jones

about the powers of two drops of blood that were given to King Erichthonius by Athene. However, each drop of blood was different and had different powers. The first drop of blood was from "the hallowed vein," meaning that it was from a vein of a Gorgon. Perhaps because of the lineage of the Gorgons, or because most of them were immortal, this drop of blood had the ability to stop plagues and bring those on the brink of death back to life. The other drop of blood, however, was from one of the snakes that made up the Gorgons' hair. This blood was said to be filled with the venom of snakes, and its single drop was deadly. The drops of blood either bringing life or taking it away work well as metaphors for Medusa: before she is beheaded she is a monster, much like the poison, but after she is a tool used to banish evil, like a cure for disease.

Hair and Heracles

Heracles, more popularly known as Hercules, was the most famous mythic hero of ancient Greece. Half god half man, he possessed immense strength and could hold the whole world on his shoulders. He is most known for his twelve labors, challenges he had to achieve before becoming a god and ascending to Olympus. Even such a valiant warrior as Heracles had help from the head of Medusa.

In the *Bibliotheca*, written by Pseudo-Apollodorus (previously known as Apollodorus), Heracles needed to win the respect of Cepheus, a king. To do so, Athene presented Heracles with a lock of Medusa's hair, or more accurately, a snake from Medusa's head. He then gave this "lock of hair" to Sterope, Cepheus's daughter, in a bronze jar. The hair had the same ability to protect as Medusa's head. When Sterope's home, Tegea, was about to be sacked by invaders, she brought out the snake, careful not to look at it, and showed it to the army once, twice, three times. Its protection turned back the invaders and Tegea was saved. When Cepheus heard that Heracles had given Sterope a snake from the head of Medusa, he welcomed Heracles into his kingdom.

A Drip from the Kibisis

Not all of the stories about Medusa's magical gifts had good aspects. There was a definite reason why the nymphs gave Perseus such a special sack to keep Medusa's head safe. As we know from the *Ion*, not only was the face of Medusa deadly but her blood was so powerful it could create life just from falling to the ground—and that is exactly what happened. As Perseus was flying back from the lonely Gorgon island, passing the great ocean, the kibisis began to fill with blood. Soon, it soaked through the silver cloth, and just as Perseus flew over Libya, a single drop fell onto the desert sand. Snakes erupted from the sand, poisonous and deadly. Medusa's blood was said to be responsible for bringing snakes to Libya. One of these snakes later killed a prophet named Mopsus.

Medusa is known as the mother of snakes.

The Birth of Pegasus

Often overlooked in the story of Perseus is the striking and strange births that occur. One of these births is a particular creature that has also frequented legends, myths, and modern day retellings: the flying horse

A flowery depiction of Pegasus's birth by Filippo Falciatore

Pegasus. As Perseus delivers Medusa's deathblow, Pegasus and his rider Chrysaor spring from her severed neck. Some stories differ on this depiction, however, and say that Pegasus and Chrysaor sprout from the Gorgon's blood that had fallen to the ground. In either case, it is revealed that Medusa is pregnant with the horse and rider. Apparently carrying the children since her encounter with Poseidon, they have stayed captive inside her until Perseus cuts her open, and they finally come flying out of her throat.

As strange as it sounds to have children born from the neck, Greek myths often had very unusual births—Athene, for example, was born from a headache, and pushed herself from Zeus's forehead. Another remarkable part of this story is that Chrysaor was born with a golden sword, which he raised as he rode Pegasus all the way to Olympus.

Links and Lineage

Pegasus, seen as a creature of heroes and connected to the Muses and the arts, is further evidence that perhaps Medusa is not as evil as she seems. Lineage played a very important part in Greek mythology: a hero was usually the child of a god; a king became a ruler because of his parentage. Both Pegasus and Chrysaor appear in Greek mythology as figures of justice, which begs the question: How can Medusa be truly evil if she has children who are champions of good?

Historians React to Pegasus's Birth

While most of the story of Medusa was something that rationalists had little trouble explaining in non-magical terms, the birth of Pegasus from Medusa's neck was a bit more difficult to interpret. It was one thing to make Medusa a caretaker of a statue (see Chapter 1), but it was quite another to say she had given birth to a horse.

Historians added their own perspectives to the story, and viewed the gruesome birth as something quite different. The birth of Chrysaor and Pegasus could actually be a record of a volcano erupting. The pair travel straight up to Olympus, a mountain much like a long inactive volcano. Chrysaor carries a gleaming golden sword in his hand. Some say that this gleaming gold actually could be Greeks recording the gleam of molten lava from far away. Pegasus might represent rocks or gas going up into the air. Their strangely explosive birth also adds some credence to the story. Herman Melville's translation of Ovid's *Metamorphoses* reads: "While deep sleep held fast Medusa and her snakes, he [Perseus] severed her head clean from her neck; and from their mother's blood swift-flying Pegasus and his brother [Chrysaor] sprang."

The word "sprang" appears over and over again in Greek and Roman texts, letting the readers know how swiftly, or even explosively, Chrysaor and Pegasus were born. A few historians have even considered relating Medusa to the story, saying that her snake hair would be similar to the look of rivers of flowing lava.

5

THE WINGED HORSE

"When the Mousai (Muses) sang, heaven, the stars, the sea and rivers stood still, while Mount Helikon, beguiled by the pleasure of it all, swelled skyward till, by the will of Poseidon, Pegasos [sic] checked it by striking the summit with his hoof."

ANTONINUS LIBERALIS, *METAMORPHOSES* 9, TRANS. CELORIA

IF MEDUSA IS THE MOST FAMOUS MONSTER of Greek mythology, then Pegasus is surely one of its best-known heroes. Pegasus is the most well-known winged horse of Greek myth, and is represented many times over through Western cultures. His name conjures images of a strong, white steed, ready to save those in danger and fight off any enemy. He flies through the air, flapping angel-like wings and running across the clouds. He has been used many times as an emblem for the arts, creativity, and speed. But what do we really know about this famous creature?

Poseidon, Father of Horses

Opposite: Pegasus and Hermes in *La Parnasse* by Andrea Mantegna

Poseidon, also known as Neptune, was the brother of Zeus and Hades and one of the most powerful Greek gods. Poseidon was the god of

Poseidon, or Triton in Roman mythology, was the god of horses.

water and controlled everything from rain clouds to wells to the vast seas. He was also known as Earth-Shaker and was given credit for any earthquakes the ancient Greeks experienced.

Poseidon was also strongly associated with horses. The horse symbolized Poseidon, and the ancient Greeks thought horses were the best animals to sacrifice to Poseidon for a safe journey across the seas. Why would a god of the sea be so closely tied to horses? The power and speed of horses is similar to the power and speed of the ocean's waves. Roy Campbell, a twentieth-century South African poet, wrote a poem called "Horses on the Camargue," which explains how Poseidon's power over the sea and his relation to horses are similar:

> I heard a sudden harmony of hooves,
> And, turning, saw afar
> A hundred snowy horses unconfined
> The silver runaways of Neptune's car
> Racing, spray-curled, like waves before the wind.

In these few lines, Campbell describes the sea foam as "a hundred snowy horses," that have the speed and ability to travel, like a car.

It is even said that Poseidon himself created horses. One myth says that Poseidon struck his trident into the ground and from this **fissure** sprang the very first horse, Areion (the Greek word for "warlike"). Areion had the body of a horse, but had the gift of speech and half of his feet were human. Despite this, he was as fast as the wind. Poseidon gave Areion to the mortal hero Adrastos, in order to help conquer Thebes. Areion lived for many years and helped many heroes of the time, eventually becoming the horse of Heracles.

It was therefore no surprise when Pegasus was born to Poseidon. In fact, according to some tales, Poseidon had several children who turned out to be horses with supernatural powers. He is often depicted in art riding a hippocamp, a beast that has the head and body of a horse but the tail of a large fish.

A Powerful Kick

Pegasus had a strong association with water. This was not just because of his lineage or the relationship between horses and water that the Greeks created. Unlike his father, who in later years was only credited with dominion over the sea, Pegasus was a creature of fresh water. Even his name, Pegasus, suggests his connection to water, as *pegai* is the ancient Greek word for "spring," or water coming up from the ground.

Pegasus kicking Mount Helicon

His connection to water is more than just his name. For many years, Pegasus roamed the world untamed. Eventually, he came to live on Helicon, the mountain of the Muses. At the top of Mount Helicon, Pegasus touched down and struck the mountain with his hoof. Here a fountain of water sprung from the earth and created the spring Hippocrene. Legend has it that anyone who drank from the waters of Hippocrene would become a great musician or poet.

Why Wings?

Of all the supernatural horses in myths, Pegasus is so well remembered because of his wings and his ability to fly. Because he was large enough to carry humans, Pegasus represented one of the few ways that Greeks could envision flying. There were many stories of humans trying to fly, most notably the tragedy of Icarus. Icarus's father made him a set of wings with wax and feathers large enough so he could fly. Icarus loved the ability to fly, but one day he flew too close to the sun. The sun warmed the wax and melted the wings, and Icarus plummeted to his death. However, a magical horse that was also a child of the gods would not be so **perilous**. Any person who could convince Pegasus to let him or her ride him would be able to soar the skies.

Many believed at the time that the higher one was, the closer one was to the gods. The gods either lived in the sky or at the top of a mountain, above the clouds, as high as possible. The highest of all these gods was Zeus, who controlled the skies. He was the most powerful god on Olympus. Pegasus's ability to fly to the tops of mountains on wings signifies how important he is. His wings are what let the readers and listeners of his stories know that he is **divine**, or godly.

Fulgentius, a medieval bishop who lived in Northern Africa, wrote in his *Mythologies* that Pegasus's wings gave him metaphorical and literal perspective. He writes: "Pegasus, for *pegaseon,* that is, an everlasting fountain. The wisdom of a good **counsel** is an everlasting fountain. So, too, is Pegasus winged, because he looks down on the whole nature of the world with a swift perception of its designs." Literally, Pegasus can fly above the ground. Metaphorically, Pegasus can detach himself from the problems of everyday life and become an impartial observer.

Muses

Muses, also known as the Pierides, were the Greek goddesses of art and culture. There were nine Muses, and each one represented a different pursuit: history, Clio; comedy, Thalia; tragedy, Melpomene; astronomy, Urania; poetry, Calliope; music, Euterpe; singing, Polyhymnia; love songs (only music dealing with marriage and love), Erato; and dancing, Terpsichore. Their mother, Mnemosyne, was the goddess of memory, and was said to remember details of important events, even back to the time before the gods, when the Titans ruled the world.

Muses were goddesses, but they did not live on Olympus. They settled on Helicon, and it was there that Pegasus stamped his foot and created the Hippocrene. They often danced around the Hippocrene and spent their time enjoying and creating beautiful music, drama, and poetry.

Many people know of the Muses as the inspiration of the works of the Grecian artists. Hesiod, a great storyteller, was supposed to have met the Muses on Helicon, where they gave him the gift of song. Some think that Muses did not make their own work but rather inspired work in others. This is not true. Muses were the greatest artists of all, and they guarded their reputation jealously. Once the bard Thamyris foolishly boasted that he had a better voice than the Muses and could out-sing every one of them. Enraged, the Muses took away Thamyris's singing and storytelling talents, and then blinded him for his shortsighted arrogance.

PEGASUS AND BELLEROPHON

"And so mighty Bellerophon reached out and put the soothing charm about the winged horse's muzzle, and subdued it."
PINDAR, *OLYMPIAN 13*, TRANS. ANTHONY VERITY

PEGASUS WAS A WILD HORSE THAT traveled freely between the mortal world and the realm of the gods. He was bound to no one, and refused to become a beast of burden. In his myth he became a valiant symbol of justice, a hero. This is the story of how the proud Pegasus was tamed.

Bellerophon

According to legend, long ago, when monsters still roamed the earth, a handsome prince named Bellerophon was born. He was brave and honorable, but tragically he was exiled from his homeland, Ephyra. Though he was separated from his family and lost his crown, he kept a sunny disposition. The fame of his honorable deeds had

Opposite: Pegasus and Bellerophon fight the deadly Chimera.

spread far and wide, and with his optimistic outlook, Bellerophon made friends quickly.

In time he came to visit King Proetus, who ruled the Tiryns. Bellerophon befriended Proetus, who quickly considered him one of his closest friends. Bellerophon was loved by all, especially Proetus's wife, Stheneboea. Stheneboea fell deeply in love with Bellerophon and one day confessed her feelings to him. Bellerophon was stunned. He could not accept her love and refused Stheneboea's advances. His refusal broke her heart. Stheneboea decided that since she could not have him, no one could. She went to her husband and told him that Bellerophon was in love with her and would not leave her alone. Proetus was furious. He wanted to order Bellerophon's execution then and there, but he reasoned he could not kill a man so loved without protests from his people.

Instead, Proetus decided to send Bellerophon away. He presented Bellerophon with a letter and asked him to bring it to King Iobates, Stheneboea's father. Bellerophon, unaware of Proetus's anger, happily agreed to deliver the message and went on his way. Favored by the gods, Bellerophon made the treacherous journey easily and was soon invited into the court of Lycia, where King Iobates ruled.

Iobates's Dilemma

Iobates was a **pious** king and never did anything to offend the gods. In his house, he strictly followed the rules of hospitality: every guest who arrived would be showered with ten days of festivals and feasts. Not until the ten days were over would Iobates ask why Bellerophon was there, and so it would be ten days until Proetus's letter would be opened.

Those ten days were filled with wonderful feasts. Bellerophon was an excellent guest, regaling his hosts with his stories of bravery and triumph. Iobates's younger daughter quickly fell for Bellerophon's handsome looks and exciting stories. Her beauty and kindness charmed Bellerophon, and by the ninth night the two were deeply in love.

As the tenth day dawned, Iobates asked for Bellerophon's letter. Unaware of anything wrong, Bellerophon willingly handed over the message. Iobates broke the seal and opened the letter. To his horror, it read, "Kill Bellerophon immediately!" Iobates knew he could not refuse his son-in-law, who was much more powerful than he was. But the rules of hospitality were clear, that once a guest is invited into the home, no harm must come to him. Iobates now had a decision to make—would he rather incur the wrath of Proetus, or the wrath of the gods?

Iobates was a shrewd thinker, as kings often have to be. He decided that it was best to incur neither. Later that day the king called Bellerophon into his hall. There, Iobates set his trap. "Bellerophon, we are so glad you have decided to visit us," he said, "You are a brave hero, and your deeds are well known. Here in Lycia, we have been plagued by a horrible monster. Will you help us, and defeat the **Chimera**?"

The Three-Headed Beast

The Chimera was a huge, three-headed monster. The first part of the Chimera was a lion, with a terrible lion head, its front legs ending in sharp claws. The body of the Chimera was that of a goat, and a gruesome goat's head sprouted from the middle of the torso, with deadly horns. The tail of the Chimera was actually

A bronze statue of the Chimera ca. 360 BCE

the body of a long, thick snake, which ended in its third head. It terrorized the countryside and the mouth of the goat breathed fire, and some said that the reptilian part of the Chimera was not merely a snake but a dragon.

Bellerophon agreed graciously, but his heart sank. He knew he could not fight the Chimera and live. If he had refused, however, he would have revealed himself a coward, and that would have brought great shame to his name.

Help from a Dream

That night Bellerophon prayed to Athene, the goddess of wisdom, to ask for help in battle. He asked to be blessed with wisdom and valor, for he would need both to defeat such a cunning beast. He stayed in the temple all night, praying to the goddess, until he finally fell asleep.

The gods had always favored Bellerophon, whose bravery and optimism had delighted them time and time again. Athene especially loved Bellerophon and heard his prayers. She would not let him die in battle against the Chimera.

As Bellerophon slept, his dream became sharper, clearer, and a beautiful woman appeared on the steps of the temple. It was Athene. "Bellerophon, you cannot win a battle against the Chimera standing on the ground," she said, frowning, "but you can defeat it from the skies."

Confused, Bellerophon asked, "How can I battle in the skies? I do not have wings to fly!"

Athene smiled down upon him. "Perhaps you do not. But I know a horse who does."

At this, Bellerophon felt a surge of excitement. As a young boy, he had dreamed to tame Pegasus, the winged horse, and had spent much of his young adulthood trying to find the beast. Could it be that Athene was offering to help him in his dream? For the first time since he had accepted his quest, Bellerophon felt hope.

Indeed, the help of Pegasus was exactly what Athene meant. In her hands appeared a harness spun from gold. She gave it to Bellerophon and told him to sacrifice a white bull to the god of horses, Poseidon. Then she disappeared, and Bellerophon woke by the altar, the golden harness in his hand.

The next day, Bellerophon sacrificed a bull, just as Athene said. He made a shrine to Athene, thanking her for her help and guidance. Then he was off to find Pegasus and begin his quest.

Flying Horses and Chimeras

In his dream, Athene had given Bellerophon a vision of Pegasus at the spring of Peirene. Bellerophon went to the clear spring, which was calm and empty. Undaunted, Bellerophon hid himself and waited quietly behind a rock, trying not to make any noise. The sun continued its path in the sky, and still Bellerophon waited patiently.

In late afternoon, he heard the sound of wings flapping against the wind, like the sound of a large bird. He peeked over the rock. Pegasus had landed, his long neck bent as he took a drink from the spring. Slowly, Bellerophon got up from the rock and snuck behind the white horse. He lifted the golden harness calmly. Then

The battle between Bellerophon and the Chimera lasted for hours.

he quickly brought it over Pegasus's head. Amazed, the horse stood still a moment. Then he looked at Bellerophon kindly, and the magic of the harness worked quickly, for he was tamed.

Off the pair flew, over the countryside. With Pegasus at his side, Bellerophon was unstoppable. Pegasus dodged every flame of the Chimera, and Bellerophon's aim was swift and true. The two fought the monster through the skies, smoke mixing with the clouds. Then, Bellerophon forced a lump of lead into the Chimera's mouth, which the monster melted with its hot breath, swallowing and choking to death.

Bellerophon Returns

Triumphant, Bellerophon and Pegasus flew back to Iobates to regale him with tales of their victory. Iobates smiled and thanked them for their help, but was secretly horrified to see them back alive. What was he to do? Bellerophon only grew in popularity for killing the Chimera.

Twice more Iobates asked Bellerophon to complete tasks that he felt would surely kill the young hero. Unfortunately for Iobates, he did not count on the help of Pegasus and the love of the gods. Iobates then sent his men to kill Bellerophon while he slept, but Bellerophon, assuming they were robbers, killed them.

After this last failure to kill Bellerophon, Iobates realized that the younger man was favored by the gods and gave up on enacting Proetus's deadly orders. He accepted Bellerophon as a worthy friend and warrior, and agreed to the marriage of Bellerophon and his youngest daughter. He later made Bellerophon heir to his kingdom.

Pride Comes Before a Fall

Pegasus bucked in pain from the bite of the gadfly.

Though the story of the Chimera is a victory for Bellerophon, his tale does not end there. Sadly, the hero who defeated so many fell victim to his own success. Bellerophon's cheerful optimism grew to **hubris**, a foolish pride that leads many heroes in Greek myths to their own destruction. Bellerophon began to think that because he had defeated so many, he was equal to the gods.

Greek gods firmly believed that mortals were inferior to them. The stories of Medusa and Athene or Thamyris and the Muses show just how angry gods became when mortals decided they were better than the gods. Bellerophon was unique in that he thought he was a god. One day he jumped on Pegasus, determined to fly up to the top of Olympus, and take his rightful place in the **pantheon** of the gods.

Now it was Zeus who became angry. Zeus was the god of thunder and lightning, and was the leader of all the gods who lived in the cloud heaven of Olympus. He was annoyed by Bellerophon's presumption, but he wanted an appropriate punishment for such pride. To waste a lightning bolt on killing a mortal would be too much trouble. Bellerophon needed to learn a deadly lesson in humility. So instead of a lightning bolt, Zeus sent a gadfly to stop Bellerophon in his tracks. The fly zoomed down and bit Pegasus hard. Pegasus reared and bucked in pain, and Bellerophon was thrown from his back, falling to his death.

CONVENNE REGE AVER, CHE DISCERNESSE
– DELLA VERA CITTADE ALMEN LA TORRE.
XVI, 95.

7

PEGASUS RIDES ON

"Then, with nostrils wide distended,
Breaking from his iron chain,
And unfolding far his pinions,
To those stars he soared again."
EXCERPT FROM "PEGASUS IN POUND," HENRY WADSWORTH LONGFELLOW

PEGASUS, LIKE MEDUSA, PLAYS A relatively small role in his own story—in part because he has no power of speech and is presented more as an asset of Bellerophon than a hero in his own right. This often happens to mythical creatures, but even when they are minor characters, readers' imaginations are captured by the ideas of such fantastic beings.

Beyond Bellerophon

While Pegasus is most famous for his fight against the Chimera and his companion Bellerophon, his story does not end with the dreaded gadfly. Even as Bellerophon fell to his end, Pegasus continued his

Opposite: Helios rides across the sky with the Hippoi Athanatioi, his winged horses.

flight and emerged above the clouds, reaching Olympus. No god blamed the horse for Bellerophon's mistake, and they were happy for him to rejoin them in their heavenly home.

Zeus was especially pleased, for though he was quick to anger, his anger soon passed. He was enchanted by the flying horse, and decided to keep him as his own. Pegasus was given a stable in the heavens and drew a chariot full of lightning and thunder for Zeus to use at his leisure. Some believed this only made sense: the son of Poseidon, the god of rain, now carried the lightning bolts of a thunderstorm.

The Poet's Horse

Not only is Pegasus one of the most loved creatures of mythology, but he is also one of the most common mythical creatures mentioned in verse. Many books of poetry are named after Pegasus, and the winged horse appears frequently in poems. Even Shakespeare mentioned Pegasus in his play *Henry IV*: "As if an angel dropped down from the clouds, / To turn and wind a fiery Pegasus / And witch the world with noble horsemanship."

As discussed in Chapter 5, Pegasus was closely associated with the Muses and the talents they signified. Pegasus's creation of Hippocrene, the spring on Helicon, cemented this connection. Greek artists honored Pegasus for his relationship to the creative talents, and as time passed Pegasus became a symbol of poets and verse. Perhaps this is because of the strong influence of Greek writings on western culture, or simply because poets liked the idea of a wild, winged horse, but this connection only strengthened with time. While other figures in Greek mythology faded from memory, Pegasus became more recognizable.

Poets began to use Pegasus to symbolize how much people appreciated poetry by writing about the state of the mythical horse. Henry Wadsworth Longfellow once wrote a poem titled "Pegasus in Pound." In it, Pegasus is captured, thrown in a prison, and then breaks free. He is unable to be bound by the villagers who captured him, just as art and creation cannot be tied down and held still, even by those in power. On the other hand, Friedrich Schiller had a much more pessimistic view of poetry and the world. He wrote "Pegasus in Yoke," in which Pegasus was sold to a poor poet and forced to work in the fields, bound to pulling carts and ploughs.

Mythic Horses Beyond Greece

Though Pegasus is most famous for his wings, horses themselves were important to the peoples of the early world. Horses were the fastest way to travel over land, and represented power, both on the battlefield and on the farm. While Pegasus was one of the few winged horses in mythology, tales from around the world tell of horses with special powers and abilities. In China, the story of the Ta Yuan horses, who flew without the aid of wings, dates back to the first century BCE, while the Nordic stories of the Vikings tell of an eight-legged horse named Sleipnir, the steed of the god Odin.

Al-Borak (or Al-Buraq), a legend from Islamic texts, is another famous winged animal, though it would be an oversimplification to say that he was a horse with wings. In fact, the Borak was a mythical beast with a woman's face, a donkey's ears, the body of a horse, and the tail of a peacock. The beautiful creature had a coat of pure white, though its wings, mane, and tail were full of jewels. Its breath smelled as wonderful as perfume.

Al-Burak is one of the most famous flying "horses."

Al-Borak was so fast that he carried the prophet Muhammad to Jerusalem and back to Mecca before a drop of water fell out of an overturned jug. He was the steed of Jibril, also known as the angel Gabriel, and it is said that Al-Borak returned to carry Muhammad to heaven when he died.

Pegasus Today

Pegasus continues to spring to mind when we think of travel, creativity, or goodness. He is a constant symbol of swift transportation, and his image has been used in logos for both the Mobil Oil Company and Pegasus Airlines. Pegasus Airlines' planes fly through the air, while cars get power from the gasoline bought at Mobil's pumps.

If you watch the beginning of a TriStar Pictures film, you will see Pegasus galloping across the skies and spreading his wings. He is the logo of the film company, reminding viewers that he is connected to the creative arts, and that perhaps the film they are about to see is worthy of the gods. Pegasus and other winged horses have shown up in many films, including *Fantasia* (1940); Disney's *Hercules* (1988), though he actually plays the part of his half-brother, Areion; *Harry Potter and the Order of the Phoenix* (2007), and *Clash of the Titans* (1981 and 2010).

The importance of horses has changed significantly in today's world. They are no longer needed for transportation, weapons of war, or workers on the farm. The horse has been replaced by the car, the tank, and the tractor. However, people's relationship to horses is still strong. Horses are considered one of the noblest creatures on Earth and are an essential part of myths and fairy tales alike. Who ever heard of a prince riding anything other than a steed?

The TriStar film company uses Pegasus as its logo.

Humanity has achieved its lofty goal of flight with innovation and technology, airplanes and spaceships, but the appeal of riding a winged horse keeps the myth of Pegasus alive. Today, no monsters roam the earth, and no horses fly in the skies. Yet the idea of riding such an untamable and elusive creature sparks our imaginations. Pegasus is not just a creature of fantasy but a myth, a symbol. From his curious birth from Medusa's head to his heroic deeds, Pegasus persists as a symbol of good springing from evil. Despite the centuries that have passed, the stubborn, wild horse still represents art, glory, and triumph in today's society. His legacy will continue to span the ages and enthrall imaginations.

A family of winged horses flies through the skies in Disney's *Fantasia*.

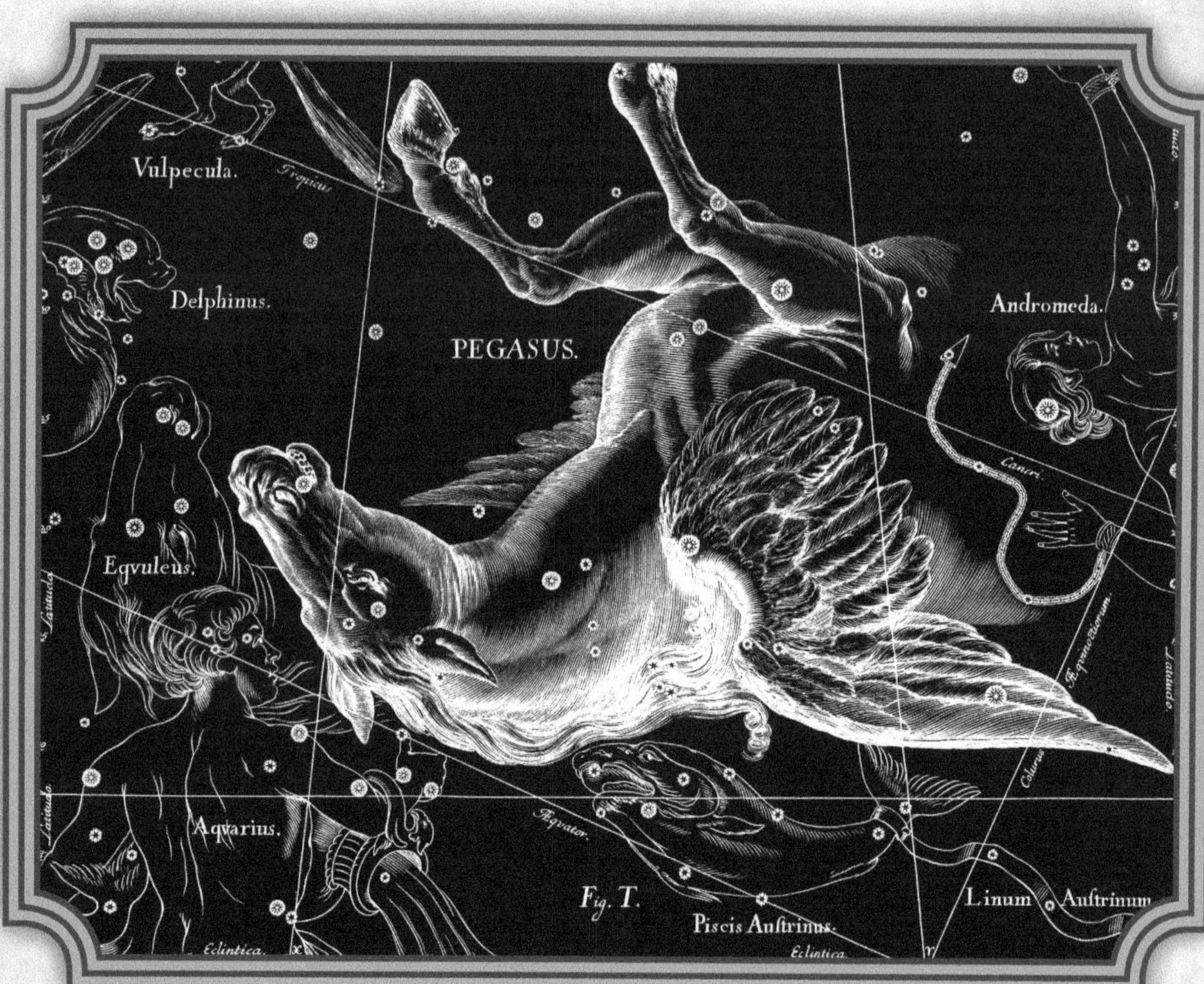

Pegasus rides through the sky for all to see.

The Horse in the Stars

It is said that after many years, Pegasus retired from carrying Zeus's thunderbolts. In honor of his service, and because he was so loved by the gods, Zeus put him up in the skies, where he could fly for all eternity.

The **constellation** of Pegasus is one of the largest groups of stars in the sky. Ptolemy, one of the greatest Greek astronomers, cataloged it as one of the first forty-eight constellations in the second century CE. The horse is made up of nine separate stars, and is well known for what is called the Great Square of Pegasus, which is the shape of four stars that make up the horse's body. The brightest star in the constellation, called Enif, forms Pegasus's nose.

For the Greeks, Pegasus rising in the sky signaled that warmer months were on their way, and the blooming of spring. Most appropriately for a horse that carried thunderbolts, the appearance of Pegasus's constellation also meant the rainy season was about to begin. The constellation of Pegasus is located in the northern sky, which means that above the equator, he is seen from late summer until early autumn, and below the equator, he appears in late winter and stays through spring.

Glossary

awestruck Filled with feelings of wonder and fear.
Chimera Mythical creature that is part lion, part goat, and part snake.
constellation A group of stars that form a pattern or image.
counsel Advice given to someone.
crone An old woman, often with magical powers.
divine Of the gods.
epic A long work (usually a poem) about the history and heroes of a particular culture or country; epics usually celebrate a people's glorious history.
extrapolate To conclude something from the facts that are given.
fissure A crack or narrow opening.
frieze A sculptured or ornamental band that wraps around a building, as decoration.
Gorgon One of three sisters, said to be so ugly that looking at them would turn the viewer to stone.
hubris A foolish amount of pride, often leading to a person's downfall, especially in Greek myths.
mythic hero A person who meets a majority of the twenty-two criteria set down by Lord Raglan in *The Hero: A Study in Tradition, Myth and Drama*, including hero is a son of god, is victorious against monsters, and becomes king.
mythology A particular culture's body of myths: stories about deities, the origins of the world and of people, and other sacred or deeply meaningful subjects.
oracle A wise person through whom the gods speak.
pantheon A grouping of gods, sometimes a temple in which gods gather.
perilous Dangerous, something likely to cause pain, injury, or death.
personify To represent (a thing or idea) as a person or as having human qualities or powers.
petrified Turned to stone.
pious Religious and devout.
polytheistic Religious belief that there are multiple gods.
rationalist A member of the Greek philosophy that believed all questions could be answered with logic and reason.
sigil A sign, word, or device said to have great power.
steadfast Firmly devoted to a belief.

To Learn More About Medusa and Pegasus

Books

d'Aulaire, Ingri and Edgar Parin d'Aulaire. *D'Aulaires' Book of Greek Myths*. New York: Delacorte Press, 1962.

Nardo, Don. *Monsters*. San Diego, CA: Lucent Books, 2002.

Vinge, Joan D. *The Random House Book of Greek Myths*. New York: Random House, 1999.

Website

Theoi Greek Mythology
www.theoi.com
Theoi is an excellent encyclopedia of Greek and Roman mythology and includes excerpts and citations of each instance a mythic character appears in ancient literature.

Video

Greek Gods
www.history.com/topics/ancient-history/greek-mythology
Check out the History Channel's overview of the Greek gods and goddesses in this animated video.

Bibliography

Atsma, Aaron J., ed. Theoi Greek Mythology. n.d. Accessed December 2014. www.theoi.com.

Bulfinch, Thomas. *Bulfinch's Mythology: The Age of Fable, The Age of Chivalry, Legends of Charlemagne*. New York: Thomas Y. Crowell, 1970.

Coolidge, Olivia. *Greek Myths*. Boston: Houghton Mifflin, 1977.

Eason, Cassandra. *Fabulous Creatures, Mythical Monsters, and Animal Power Symbols*. Westport, CT: Greenwood Press, 2008.

Garber, Marjorie, and Nancy J. Vickers. *The Medusa Reader*. New York: Routledge, 2003.

Hamilton, Edith. *Mythology: Timeless Tales of Gods and Heroes*. New York: Grand Central Publishing, 1969.

Kaplan, Mark. *Medusa's Gaze and Vampire's Bite: The Science of Monsters*. New York: Scribner, 2012.

Manton, Jo, and Robert Gittings. *The Flying Horses: Tales from China*. New York: Holt, Rinehart and Winston, 1977.

March, Jenny. *The Penguin Book of Classical Myths*. London: Penguin Books, 2008.

Matthews, John, and Caitlin Matthews. *The Element Encyclopedia of Magical Creatures*. New York: Harper Element, 2005.

Murray, Alexander S. *Who's Who in Mythology*. New York: Bracken Books, 1988.

O'Connell, Mark, and Raje Airey. *The Complete Encyclopedia of Signs and Symbols*. London: Hermes House, 2006.

Pindar. *The Complete Odes*. Translated by Anthony Verity. Oxford, England: Oxford University Press, 2007.

Pinsent, John. *Myths and Legends of Ancient Greece*. New York: Grosset & Dunlap, 1970.

Tripp, Edward. *Crowell's Handbook of Classical Mythology*. New York: Thomas Y. Crowell, 1970.

Zimmermann, Kim Ann. "Pegasus Constellation: Facts and Notable Features." Space.com. July 24, 2012. www.space.com/16743-constellation-pegasus.html.

Index

Page numbers in **boldface** are illustrations. Entries in **boldface** are glossary terms.

About the Author

Amy Hayes studied creative writing and children's literature at the University of Pittsburgh. As a young child, she was surrounded by works of Greek mythology, which captured her imagination. She now lives in the lovely city of Buffalo, New York.